charlies poem

BY

roy thomas dow

illustrations by james o'reilly

PRESS

charlies poem
© copyright Roy T. Dow 2019 All rights reserved.

No part of this book may be used or reproduced by any means, graphic, electronic or mechanical, including photocopying, recording, taping or by any information storage retrieval system without the written permission of the author except in the case of brief quotations embodied in critical articles and reviews.

(First Published by Balboa Press in 2019)

This edition exclusively published by 1331PRESS in June 2022

1331 press, c/o
Roy (Thomas Dow)
PO Box 228
Wondai
Qld 4606 Australia
Details may be found on roydow.com

General Disclaimer.
This is a work of fiction, to sow seeds of change.
The publisher, author and god apologise for any offence or distress caused by the content of this work.

Editing, layout & design, in house

ISBN: 978-1-922499-06-6 (Print Book)
ISBN: 978-1-922499-05-9 (E-Book)
ISBN: TBC   (Audible Book)

See the 1331PRESS page at roydow.com for details.

1331 press.   Rev. Date: 0206-2022.

Preface

Charlies Poem is perhaps the greatest challenge one could set for the human race,
Within these pages, a tale is told of the most impossible proportions, impossible hopes and dreams. Something that just could never BE. Save a miracle...

I believe, this challenge is here to call out the revolution on the evolution of the human animal, the BEan, through the single revolution of this planet, as we strive to force equality on a desensitised world.

DaVinci said, "Simplicity is the ultimate sophistication." Look around at how complicated we are!

Here are the seeds for the beginnings of the ultimate simplicity.
One of co-operation, of sharing. Of care and assistance. Of equality across the board.

Moves to change the world are always taking place, for this awareness (which is all there is), is a dynamic environment. Organic even; as we interact with all, without. As we progress in our expanding of awareness, questions of fair and right come to the fore.
Time to focus on a different purpose!

In this new world of equality, there can be no class separation or successions of any kind. All of us have the same goal, the same purpose. Many are here to guide humanity towards the necessary changes to evolve. Participation remains a choice!

A wave of intent will be recognised and will ovverwhelm all who oppose this most natural transition. Such is the *power of love*.

Judgment is coming. Do you believe? Can you see? This judgement will determine your next experience.
You cannot BEcome, what you do not BElieve, after all!

Read on, and be challenged.
It's time to embrace the future!

Roy T Dow 01062022 - Qld Australia

Other titles in the 'charlies' series

charlies guide

charlies poem

charleis plan

charlies way

All titles published <u>exclusively</u>,

by 1331PRESS

PRESS

"Is it true?" asked charlie hopefully,
as he walked towards the door.
"Is it true that we're all equal now,
and no such thing as poor?"

His dad was clearing up his clothes,
all strewn across the floor.
'Are we all sharing everything,
no money anymore?'

"We were never really destitute,
we were better off than some.
With faith in god and love of life,
I new the food would come."

"But as for money, yes, it's gone,
although it made some numb.
Apparently, somebody said,
that using it was dumb."

Charlie thought on what was said,
and opened up the door.
"Let's go and check it out then dad,"
"We'll go to *old rabs store*"

"Ok let's go, i'll get my keys,
we'll go down in the car.
I known that we could walk there
and it isn't very far"

"But afterwards we'll carry on,
and go down into town,
and see if everyone's gone mad
and lootings going down."

Charlie stopped and grinned a bit,
then looked up at his dad.
"Looting, stealing, surely not.
Is freely sharing bad?"

"If I see someone crying,
cos they haven't got enough,
I just open up my heart,
and give them lots of stuff."

"Of course, of course,' his dad said.
"Think of sharing and be kind.
It's hard to get the old
barbaric ways out of your mind."

"I hope there isn't fighting,
all the people going mad.
I really should be positive.
I really should be glad."

"Will everybody realise
that there is no need to hoard?
For that's the truth, it sets us free.
And that's the true reward."

They gathered up some things to take,
and put them in the car.
Dad liked to plan for *just in case*,
although it wasn't far.

With beaming smiles, they both set off,
to see how they would fair.
In the rebirth of their eden.
In gods garden where we share.

And so, we start the tale, of
how the whole world woke to find,
That everyone was finding love,
and being really kind.

The natural stuff inside us all,
is yearning to be free.
You'll always find love deep inside
the likes of you and me.

So turn the page and lets go forth,
and see how things evolve.
Of how our love will change the world
and see despair dissolve.

Of how the poorest in the land,
will always lend an ear.
And help that little group that *have*,
to rid themselves of *fear*.

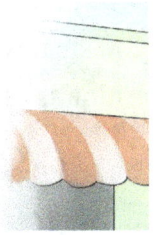

Outside *old rabs,* there was no queue,
no people stood in line.
Charlies dad, he parked the car,
and everything looked fine.

They both got out and went inside,
to see if it was true.
Has truth and common sense prevailed,
the messages got through?

Inside the shop the shelves had stuff,
there seems no looting here.
Why would you steal when all is free?
The question is quite clear.

"It's the olden's, talking common sense,
a smile a wink a nudge.
Take it, if you *need* it,
here's some chocolate and some fudge"

Rab shared the news, the tales of joy,
the words from all the sages.
Born of the lives, of truth and years,
and shared within these pages.

Of how the plan to take control,
was truly born of love.
Extended hands to guide the young,
as peaceful as a dove.

In truth it is towards us all,
for each of us can err.
Find forgiveness in your heart,
forgiveness that we share.

It saves us from our wanton greed's,
our selfishness and lusts,
That really are redundant now,
this ain't no boom or bust.

~*~

An idea simmered, in our heads,
a realisation grew,
That this might be the only chance,
for saving me and you.

About 6 billion souls or more,
as souls the system claims,
About to find their freedom,
and dissolve financial chains.

That is, the one reality,
the truth that sets us free.
And YES, THIS IS, OUR CHOICE,
our CHANCE. It's easy, 1 2 3.

Grow faith to burn the fires bright,
that make this earth revolve,
As people opened up their hearts,
and let their fears dissolve.

If each of us take all we need,
and then we take no more,
We'll never fear the stampedes
as we open up the door.

Rab shared the tales,
He shared the love,
He shared it all for free.
Became the man he dreamed to be,
For everyone to see

So charlie and his dad they left,
and drove down into town.
Neither could stop smiling,
and neither one could frown.

It seemed the truth had turned to love,
and happiness then grew.
First you trust yourself to share,
The same as others do.

They took just what they needed,
and left the other things.
Identifying worthless stuff,
like watches, gold and rings.

Some food and a new jacket,
some underpants and socks,
No one needs those sparkly things.
The silly polished rocks.

So much waste about to end,
a planet we can love.
The crazy things we thought we needed,
now it's just a dove.

So on with every second,
every inch and every smile.
As new light dawns on every soul,
growing all the while.

When charlie and his dad were done,
they went back home for lunch.
Well maybe, it's too early, so
we'll have to call it brunch.

With tuck consumed, relaxed they were,
upon the sofa curled.
They witnessed all the truth unfold,
the tv tracked the world.

In france there was the guillotine,
and revolution came.
Yet this time no one lost their head,
the river kept them sane.

While most just shrugged their shoulders,
ate bread and cheese, drank wine,
Some more just puffed 'Abe Lincolns Weed',
they knew things would be fine.

The truth was really dawning,
on the billions who looked on.
To see if all were playing fair,
and singing the same song.

The truth was, it was working,
with the rising of the sun.
And all, it seemed, in light and love,
their hearts were overrun.

To see such change in energy,
to feel such hearts desire.
Growing in expectancy,
revolving round the fire.

The measures of excitement,
well they grew and didn't stop.
The boundless love and childlike glee,
it caught us on the hop.

Fears are being put aside,
first you must believe.
Understand the truth and see,
there's nothing here to grieve.

Give everyone a shelter,
A home, safe warm and free.
A feeling of belonging,
in the true community.

In africa the foods poured in,
with medicines and love.
The origin of miracles
is not just from above.

The greatest acts of love, as seen,
by all you hooman beans,
was when each of you *woke* and *chose*
(*with love*), *to live your dreams.*

So many people out of work,
it's now the time to start.
To share the land for all our good,
the old ways now depart.

Free food, accommodation,
we can build and grow at pace,
It's all that any hoobean needs,
to start and win the race.

Every bean will do their bit,
it all begins with you,
If you, yes you, look after you,
then surely I will to.

Cos i'm a me, I mean an I,
and surely, you're the you,
So, you do your bit,
I'll do mine, the plan we'll follow through.

The brits, the french and africans,
and on the plain in spain.
All influenced the dutch and danes,
and everyone the same.

Anyone resisting, was
politely left alone.
Historic and amazing scenes,
were even seen in rome.

The pope got up, and dressed himself,
then made himself some toast.
Shuddered in a retrospective,
found no need to boast.

Again, a need, a place is filled,
by shepherds full of love.
Decide to trust themselves again,
and love like god above.

The single most important truth,
that everyone can see,
We're free to build and grow our faith,
for g we cannot see.

Is it so wrong for every
single person on this earth,
To *choose* their life at *every* step?
all life has equal worth.

Islamic guides could not contain,
the glee of those set free.
To leave the homeland, know you can,
a free life beckons thee.

Tis true, some guides they also ran,
a new life theirs to claim.
And it's a life for everyone,
for everyone's the same.

We all have choice, we know it's true,
what I would like to see,
You *feed* the man caught stealing,
(you **do not**, cut off his hand)

~*~

The difference is, a recognition,
of the love within.
Humility is the great anchor
of conscious thought.

So easy is this feeling,
as it sweeps across the land.

Rebalancing, the views within,
those coming from without.
We need to care for each of us,
self-love it is within.

Anyone can harbour hate,
Let inside anger grow.
Takes courage; in the mirror, truth!
The time, has come to know.

Right across the vast expanse
of mother russia grew,
That loving sense of comradeship,
it stayed because it's true.

Now standing at the signpost,
it's today that you can see,
Perspective is misleading,
as we think of you and me.

Too much time spent looking back,
our life is in today,
And every day is full of change,
because that's just life's way.

While history, it can teach us much,
can also drag us down.
Understand that truth is truth,
and change has come to town.

The middle east, it grew in love,
on that day of change.
Cos people just love loving,
and then nothings out of range.

The Indians, and all surrounds,
they all jumped on with glee.
Cos loving's so infectious,
for the likes of you and me.

The Aussies, well some stumbled,
fear got them on the run.
They drowned their sorrows, fed their fears,
in whisky, beer and rum.

But mateship kept 'em standing,
and the sober ones stood fast.
Equality from coast to coast,
an Aussie dream, at last!

The far east is a land of wisdom,
full of sages wise.
What happened here I feel quite sure,
will come as no surprise.

Ideas of home and family,
of honour one can trace.
With ease the sharing carries on,
the paradigm embraced.

Across the vast pacific,
one could see the sun traverse.
Another day of light and love,
always change, not worse.

All new their needs would now be met,
with unconditional love
Guided with the feelings
of the right way from above.

Time saw the americas,
at last come into view.
The south with love embraced it all,
with no hard pill to chew.

The central regions struggled,
with brutality and fear.
The gangs and guns, took time to silence,
nothing really new.

Trumpty dumpty sat it seems,
but not upon a wall.
Tis said he had a change of heart,
no longer needs an orle.

Instead he opened up his heart,
to what his peoples need.
He planted seeds of truth and love,
on which the people feed.

Across the world it seemed, a truth
was coming into view.
Divine right is for everyone,
so that means me and you.

People moved out from the hells,
and started just next door.
To lay the stones for loving homes,
so breaking bones no more.

With green and ice lands feeling love,
earths energy has changed.
A different future beckons,
as the mindsets rearranged.

We have the choice together,
and we make it everyday.
*We **all** create the way it is,
and how we want to play.*

Rules and reg's constrain us,
we can brush them all aside,
And make decisions made with love,
and walk this earth with pride.

If WE, all say the rule is wrong,
or maybe it's just I?
Perhaps we say ok then, why not
give that thing a try?

Politics, financial houses
all gone in the bin
along with all the other stuff,
with use we'd never win

The simplest ways to make a smile,
is to your heart be true.
Always wear your truth with love,
until there's something new.

Be prepared for change and learn,
that change is all around.
"Fulfil your wishes hopes and dreams,
before you're underground".

Until the time, I know will come,
when we will never age.
And no more start a final chapter,
read a final page.

Every plan, is just a guide,
designed to make us think.
The truth is, life is fearless change,
it's always on the brink.

But change is good, mistakes are made,
just like they always are.
With all the constant changes,
we will always travel far.

I hear an echo from the past,
a brother calls me, true.
To conjure up a global change,
embracing something new.

Ignore the chains of greed,
and wipe the error from your eye.
Shed the cloak of doldrums,
spread your wings and search the sky.

I've sat with those that have so much,
and those that have so little.
I've heard the booming, boasting hearts
and felt the hearts so brittle.

In truth, I witness, here for thee,
to say the time has come.
To wave goodbye to money,
with the setting of the sun.

.

..

...

......

....

?

I took a chance at midnight,
I looked back, across the land.
I thought of how god's present.
How we feel the guiding hand.

Life is love, and love will grow,
and ever seek to change.
The growth and learning never stops,
no pre-determined range.

If each of us will understand,
the others just the same.
That age and colour have no bearing,
niether does a name.

Hold on to your humility,
with your own self be true.
The yearning for the love divine,
is growing inside you.

With shelter food and clothing,
we can tend this eden, home.
Or safely wander freely,
in gods garden we can roam.

There's nothing here to own dear beans,
tis now you see it true.
Tend the gifts inside the bag,
you always have with you.

The power's there in pictures,
expectation leads to proof.
A sanctuary, for your own creations,
fabricating truth.

The great successes of your life,
that bring you lasting peace,
Create with unconditional love.
Success will be complete.

.
..
...
......
....

?

I took a walk on planet earth,
and saw that all was good.
Had see the dream embraced by all,
Just because we could.

I looked around, I knew not
where I was, nor did I care.
Smiling, breathing easy, winds
of change blew through my hair.

A stranger stood before me,
and another by my side.
We didn't know each other,
and were hear to share the ride.

One god, one father, guide and love,
our freedom that we share.
Here stand "the ranks of those,
that live their lives without a care".

The plan was not perfection,
it was simply based on love.
I watched for years, then realsied,
all you needed was a shove.

I've more idea's and thoughts,
on how we might progress from here.
Of how our eden home is made,
with gentle step's, it's clear.

See the singularity,
the *infinite divine*
Love , creation, energy,
expression so sublime,

We'll build *a simple framework*,
as a system for success.
Our mind we change, within these pages.
Fear, we now repress.

Continue on, until the end,
Which never comes in view.
The infinite is in us all,
Just close your eyes, it waits for you.

The *water bearer* here? Tis true.
We greet another age.
Boldly walking on through time,
so turn another page.

~*~

Unconditional love to all life.
Take only, what is ours to take.

Instantly, free technologies, that assist us is in preserving the planet and facilitate ease of survival for all.

The misguided will now clearly see the error of their ways.
Everything, is available to us.

The paradigm changes, and we all join in, being completely overwhelmed with love and we just work it out, together, as one global family with zero ties.

Understand, it has taken over 25,000 years to get to this excess in error. To create the "tipping point".

Now we just say enough is enough, and we stop everything.
We **can**, truly stop, immediately.

Because we need to face truth, to see truth.
REAL TRUTH not lies (a total waste of thought).
Forget control. Power, Position.
Control Yourself.
Trust yourself,
Forgive yourself.

Do it right, based on feelings, alone.
We all know if something is right.

DO NOT FOLLOW A MAN.

Just follow your heart.
YOUR heart.

Pause, and learn to look inside.

Understand the true power of your own unconditional love,
You, are the change.

Which is infinite.

~*~

Gifts come with responsibility
Much to learn and acquire.

But the journey of bliss,
infinite creative power,
based on love
it's there for us all!

HAVE NO FEAR,
YOU ARE FREE,
AND THE BIG G LOVES YOU

ALWAYS

Less haste,
with gentle steps to progress.
Feeling the divine.

the *infinite* expression
the *infinite* creation
the *infinite* energy

the infinite *YOU*

~*~

charlie's poem, is dedicated with
unconditional love to all beans

I pray for myself, and all beans
that we may ever grow in knowing.

Ultimately,
changing ourselves, and our world.

The changes are here, now.

Mind your thoughts.
Mind your words.
Mind your actions.

roydow.com
changethwroldnow.org

Thank you for your support.

roy

1331PRESS

Books released or planned for release in 2022.

Strawberry Angel and the Bean	ebook
Charlies Poem	POD
"	ebook
Charlies Guide	POD
"	ebook
Charlies Plan (2nd edition)	POD
"	ebook
Charlies Way (2nd edition)	POD
"	ebook
Echoes from the Soul	POD
(A first Anthology)	ebook
Expanding Awareness	POD
(The End Times Guide)	ebook

Details can be found on on the 1331PRESS page at roydow.com

Also available in print
Strawberry Angel and the Bean

A love story as old as time...

Published under the name,
Roy Thomas

www.ingramcontent.com/pod-product-compliance
Lightning Source LLC
Chambersburg PA
CBHW071543080526
44588CB00011B/1771